Investigating
MASS SHOOTINGS IN THE UNITED STATES

BRIDEY HEING

Rosen
YA™

New York

Published in 2018 by The Rosen Publishing Group, Inc.
29 East 21st Street, New York, NY 10010

First Edition

Library of Congress Cataloging-in-Publication Data

Names: Heing, Bridey, author.
Title: Investigating mass shootings in the United States / Bridey Heing.
Description: First edition. | New York, NY : Rosen Publishing Group, Inc.,
2018. | Series: Terrorism in the 21st century: causes and effects |
Includes bibliographical references and index. | Audience: Grades 7–12.
Identifiers: LCCN 2016059453 | ISBN 9781508174622 (library bound : alk. paper)
Subjects: LCSH: Firearms and crime—United States—Juvenile literature. | Mass murder
United States—Juvenile literature. | Violent crimes—United States—Juvenile literature. |
Gun control—United States–Juvenile literature.
Classification: LCC HV7436 .H45 2018 | DDC 363.25/952340973—dc23
LC record available at https://lccn.loc.gov/2016059453

Manufactured in China

Contents

Introduction

n recent years, many mass shootings have occurred across the United States. These unexpected attacks have killed thousands, wounded more, and caused a heated debate on how best to put a stop to gun violence. Shootings have also created an environment of fear with many concerned that an attack could be carried out anywhere. It is perhaps one of the most pressing issues of the early twenty-first century and is one that is still far from being resolved.

While most of the country agrees we must do something to stop mass shootings, leaders haven't been able to agree on how best to tackle the problem. As a result, mass shootings have become a source of ongoing political conflict. Finding solutions has proven very difficult, and there is no end to the political stalemate in sight. As a result, we have not effectively addressed how to end mass shootings.

Although they are often not called acts of terrorism, many mass shootings can be seen as terrorist activity, which is defined as violent action meant to bring about specific change or promote a political agenda. Some shooters state their motives before an attack, although many do not. In cases when a shooter is taken into custody, a trial can be held to determine why they carried out a mass shooting in the first place. But in other cases, such as when the shooter is killed during the attack, we are left to wonder what their actions were meant to accomplish or represent.

Today the power of social media and the Internet has raised concerns about how terrorists could use US citizens to carry out attacks. Already

we've seen attackers pledge allegiance to terrorist groups, such as the Islamic State in Iraq and Syria (ISIS) or white nationalist groups, before carrying out attacks. But many of those who do so are not in direct contact with the group they seem to represent, which poses questions about how

The Sandy Hook Elementary School shooting, memorialized here, sparked a debate on gun violence in the United States.

seriously we should take their affiliation. This complicates the way we think about terrorism by making it seem as if terrorist threats are growing while also challenging what we consider to be terrorism.

Mass shootings highlight a number of related issues facing the United States, including the ongoing debate about gun rights and how to effectively protect the public while respecting the rights of individuals. These issues are important and complex, which makes finding solutions all the more difficult. On top of that, we're still trying to understand how best to fight terrorism before it takes place.

In this book, we will learn about some recent mass shootings and how they changed the public debate about gun violence, some of the issues involved in finding a solution to end mass shootings, proposed legislation and programs that could make a difference, and what experts feel the future holds for mass shootings and their link to terrorism. By looking at mass shootings from all of these angles, we'll come away with a wide understanding of what mass shootings are, what they mean, and how they might be stopped.

CHAPTER ONE

The History of Mass Shootings

While mass shootings have seemingly become more frequent in recent years, gun violence has been a part of American culture for a long time. But as technology has evolved, so has the ability

One of the largest questions in the debate on mass shootings is what role gun control can play in stopping such attacks.

of one person to inflict previously unimaginable levels of destruction and violence in a short amount of time, which has given rise to mass shootings as we know them today.

What is a Mass Shooting?

"Mass shooting" is a commonly used phrase with many meanings. There are multiple ways in which the term can be used, ranging from a large number of people killed in one attack to a large number of people wounded. According to some, there are hundreds of mass shootings in the United States each year; according to others, only a handful occur. This lack of an agreed-upon definition can make studying or even debating mass shootings difficult and has led to public debates on what attacks should be categorized in this way.

The Congressional Research Service (CRS) defines a mass shooting as an attack in which four or more people are killed with a firearm, while the Federal Bureau of Investigation (FBI) considers a mass killing (under which mass shootings fall) any attack in which three or more people are killed. But according to the Mass Shooting Tracker, a crowd-sourced website that is often cited by the media and gun-control advocates, a mass shooting is any event in which four or more people are shot, whether it results in injury or fatality. A lot of people and officials do not agree with that definition and claim that it inflates the number of mass shootings taking place to cause undue public panic. Some have also expressed that not all shootings in which multiple deaths occur should be grouped together and that the random selection of victims should also be a key facet in determining a mass shooting. Otherwise, there is no way to distinguish shootings that would be considered terrorism from those that would be considered murder committed, for example, by family members.

Another obstacle to fully understanding mass shootings—and to creating an agreed-upon definition—is that the Centers for Disease Control (CDC), the national public health institute in the United States, is not able to carry out research on gun violence. Although the agency's name suggests that it only researches diseases, the CDC studies many kinds of violence, including child abuse and deaths by suicide. But Congress passed restrictions in 1997 that stopped the CDC from spending money on researching gun violence, citing concerns that those studies could be seen as advocating for gun control. This doesn't stop the federal government from carrying out some research (the Congressional Research Service is one example of a federal organization that tracks gun violence), but it does limit our ability to get a complete picture of mass shootings.

The disagreements over what counts as a mass shooting, as well as the lack of a centralized organization keeping track of that information, leads to starkly different results. In 2013, the most recent year for which federal research has been published, the Mass Shooting Tracker counted a total of 363 mass shootings, or about one per day. By comparison, the Congressional Research Service counted only twenty-five.

Mass Shootings in US History

Although mass shootings are more common today, gun violence has played a role in US history from the early days of the country. From duels to the vigilante justice of the Wild West to mob era shootings, gun violence has taken different forms over the past few centuries. But mass shootings as we know them are largely a modern phenomenon. In the first half of the twentieth century, most large-scale shootings were related to crime or involved the shooter's family. These differ from the indiscriminate attacks we consider to be mass shootings today.

These weapons were used by Charles Whitman during his attack in 1966, the first modern mass shooting in the United States.

The history of shootings in the United States has always been closely linked with technology, particularly military technology. As guns were developed for use on the battlefield, they eventually found their way to the streets. An example of this is the famous "Tommy" submachine gun, which was developed during World War I. In the 1920s, this gun became the weapon of choice for mobsters. One of today's most controversial weapons—the semiautomatic AR-15—has been used in several high-profile shootings and was developed for use in the Vietnam War.

According to a study by *The Washington Post*, the first modern mass shooting in the United States took place in 1966, when Charles Whitman killed fourteen people at the University of Texas in Austin after shooting his wife and mother. In the decades since, the number of shootings that can broadly be considered mass shootings—meaning that they took place in public and involved four or more gunshot victims—skyrocketed. Dr. Grant Duwe, author of *Mass Murder in the United States: A History*, counts 141 mass shootings that have taken place between 1965 and 2015, while the FBI counts 160 between 2000 and 2013.

THE 1960S AND 1970S: A TURNING POINT

Gun violence has always been part of American history, but the twentieth century saw a major shift in both how guns are used and how the public debates issues surrounding guns. In the 1960s, the assassinations of President John F. Kennedy, civil rights leader

(continued on the next page)

(continued from the previous page)

The National Rifle Association (NRA) is the largest pro-gun lobbying group in the United States.

Martin Luther King Jr., and presidential candidate Robert Kennedy gave rise to more calls for gun control, which led to the passage of the Gun Control Act in 1968. It restricted the interstate trafficking of firearms and required the licensing of gun vendors. At first, gun advocates, including the National Rifle Association (NRA), were comfortable with the increased regulation. But at the group's annual conference in 1977, internal unrest led to the new leadership of Harlon Carter. Carter advocated for no compromise on gun rights, and since then the group has opposed any new legislation on firearms. This shift in policy marked a new era in our public debate on gun control that has led to today's stalemate in both public discussion and policy.

Mass Shootings as Terrorism

Mass shootings are carried out for reasons ranging from obsessive beliefs to making a political statement. Despite this, we don't often talk about mass shootings as a form of terrorism. Part of that is due to how we define terrorism and how little is often known about those who carry out mass shootings. Terrorism, according to the government, is an act of violence that is meant to further a political or ideological cause; terrorism is intended to use terror to change policy or social norms. Although we often associate terrorism with radical Islam, terrorism does not have to be

The Emanuel African Methodist Episcopal Church in Charleston, South Carolina, was the target of an attack by Dylann Roof.

religiously motivated. The kind of extremism that leads to terrorist activity can be inspired by any range of beliefs, whether they are religious or political in nature.

Since it's common for shooters to die during attacks, either at their own hand or as a result of engaging in gunfire with the police, it is not always easy to find out if they are motivated by a desire to change society or politics. In a case where a motive can be determined because the shooter targeted a specific group, such as the Wisconsin Sikh temple shooting in 2012 or the Charleston church shooting in 2015, it is often deemed a hate crime rather than an act of terrorism.

But that does not mean mass shootings cannot be acts of domestic terrorism. Although domestic terrorism is rare, it is more common than terrorism carried out by foreign nationals, and it is increasingly carried out with guns rather than other weapons. Since the September 11 terrorist attacks, 85 percent of Americans killed in terrorist attacks on US soil were victims of attackers using guns.

CHAPTER TWO

Major Mass Shootings in the United States

While all mass shootings are tragedies, some have become turning points in American gun violence. They have also sparked changes in how we think about and talk about gun violence. Although

The Columbine shooting in 1999 changed the way we talk about guns in schools and how to best protect students.

each attack has marked a shift in some way, the mass shootings detailed in this chapter were significant not just because of what occurred but also because of what they represented and how they shaped the future in terms of US policy, legislation, and public discussion.

Columbine High School

Although the shooting at Columbine High School in Columbine, Colorado, took place in 1999, its impact has shaped how we debate mass shootings in the twenty-first century. Students Eric Harris and Dylan Klebold carried out the attack on April 20, killing twelve students, one teacher, and then themselves over the course of an hour. They also injured twenty-one people.

This shooting soon became a flashpoint for the debate on mass shootings. The students who planned and carried out the attack felt they were unpopular outcasts and, according to those who survived, their sense of isolation may have determined whom they targeted. Following the attack, the public openly debated the impact of Goth culture, heavy metal music with violent imagery, bullying, and other social elements that could have had an impact on the shooters.

Although much of the concern about music and other cultural elements has faded with time, Columbine also ushered in debates about how best to provide protection for students. It was following this attack that many schools put in place greater security measures, such as metal detectors and lockdown drills. Today, such practices are a common part of the school system, but in the months following Columbine, parents, students, and school officials deliberated the impact such measures could have on the learning environment. Ultimately, many decided that children's safety justified these new policies, and the way students go to school and how schools confront the threat of shootings changed forever.

Virginia Tech

Eight years after Columbine, a shooting on the Virginia Tech campus in Blacksburg, Virginia, highlighted issues with both restrictions on access to firearms for those with potentially dangerous mental health concerns and school privacy policies. On the morning of April 16, 2007, student Seung-Hui Cho carried out a two-hour attack across two buildings on campus, killing thirty-two students and faculty and injuring seventeen. Cho killed himself during the shooting.

Cho's mental health was called into question shortly after news broke of the shooting. He had shown signs of instability and deterioration in recent months, including an incident in which he was caught stalking female students. In high school, Cho had received special accommodations due to severe anxiety and other mental health issues, none of which were addressed by his university. The shooting ignited numerous debates on the limits of personal privacy when there is reasonable concern that an individual may cause harm to themselves or others, as well as how schools can better provide access to services for students who may be struggling.

The shooting also sparked conversations about who should and can have access to firearms, specifically whether the existing background checks were substantial enough to catch past warnings. Although those with diagnosed mental illnesses are statistically more likely to be victims of mass shootings than perpetrators, the majority of attackers in mass shootings have shown signs of potential mental disorders prior to carrying out these attacks. In response to the shooting, President George W. Bush signed into law the National Instant Criminal Background Check System Improvement Act, providing greater funding to states to improve their instant background check records and tightening restrictions on who can be denied a firearm due to mental health concerns. While the bill has been controversial due to concerns that it could stigmatize or discriminate against those with mental illness, it was the first major federal gun legislation passed in over two decades.

Fort Hood

In most cases, multiple mass shootings do not occur in one location, but Fort Hood, a military base in Texas, has experienced two very different shootings. The first was in 2009, when Major Nidal Hasan killed thirteen and injured thirty. The second was in 2014, when Specialist Ivan Lopez killed four and injured fourteen before killing himself. While the second shooting occurred following a workplace fight, many considered the first a terrorist attack due to connections between Hasan and a Yemen-based suspected terrorist. Although the government did not classify the attack as a terrorist act, the shooting does highlight the issue of radicalization by foreign organizations and the threat it can pose in the United States.

Documents found after the shooting and statements made by Hasan during his trial suggest that he carried out the attack to support Islamist terrorist organizations, including the Taliban. He had been in touch via email with Anwar al-Awlaki, an American imam based in Yemen who had ties to the terrorist organization al-Qaeda prior to being killed in a drone strike. Hasan also attended a mosque where al-Awlaki preached before leaving the United States. Fellow soldiers expressed concern about his radicalization and reported after the shooting that he showed support for Islamist causes and opposition to fighting in the Middle East. During his trial, Hasan told the court that he carried out the shooting to protect Taliban leadership and argued that his actions were justified—not that he hadn't carried out the attack.

The two shootings carried out at Fort Hood called into question the role of Islamic extremism in mass shootings.

Sandy Hook

Despite the new measures that went into effect after Columbine, Sandy Hook Elementary School in Newtown, Connecticut, was the site of one of the deadliest mass shootings in US history in 2012. The shooter, Adam Lanza, killed twenty-six people, primarily six- and seven-year-old students. He killed himself before being taken into custody and had killed his mother before going to the school.

The shooting was shocking due to the extreme violence of the attack, the age of the majority of the victims, and the lack of a clear motive. Although Lanza showed signs of possible mental illness and had a fascination with guns, that alone doesn't explain why he carried out the attack. Today, experts are still unsure about Lanza's motives.

MASS SHOOTINGS AROUND THE WORLD

The United States has both the world's highest rate of gun ownership and the highest percentage of mass shootings. According to a study by University of Alabama professor Adam Lankford, the United States has around 300 million firearms, while the second highest rate of ownership—in Yemen—is just 11.5 million. Meanwhile, the United States experienced 33 percent of the world's mass shootings between 1966 and 2012, a higher percentage than any other individual country. It is not clear why mass shootings occur more often in the United States, whereas other types of large-scale civilian attacks are more rare. High gun ownership is often cited as the reason, although it is unclear if that alone is responsible for the higher rate of attacks. Despite these numbers, studies have also shown that the United States is safer overall today than it was twenty years ago and that the rate of gun violence has dropped in that time.

Sandy Hook marked a turning point in the debate on gun control with many advocates for greater regulations organizing to push for closing security loopholes before a gun can be purchased. Groups such as the Brady Campaign to Prevent Gun Violence, the Coalition to Stop Gun Violence, and Everytown for Gun Safety have become more outspoken about possible reforms since the attack on Sandy Hook. In 2013, President Obama signed twenty-three reforms into law with an executive order that ranged from steps to make state-level background checks more effective to providing better training for law enforcement officials who respond to active-shooter situations. Although these addressed some of the issues raised by advocates, Congress has not passed new laws providing more permanent solutions.

Oak Creek and Charleston

In some cases, mass shootings are hate crimes, or crimes committed against a specific population due to bias, such as racism. In recent years, two shootings are examples of how mass shootings are used to target specific groups. Both attacks were carried out at places of worship with the first against Sikhs, or followers of the Indian religion Sikhism, and the second against African Americans.

On August 5, 2012, Wade Michael Page attacked a Sikh temple in Oak Creek, Wisconsin, killing six worshippers and injuring one responding officer before killing himself. Page had ties to white supremacist and neo-Nazi groups and played in bands identified by the Southern Poverty Law Center as being racist and supporting white power. Because of these connections, the incident was investigated by state and federal agencies as a terrorist attack and hate crime, although no formal motive was released. It was believed that he acted alone rather than on behalf of a group, and he left no indication of why he targeted that specific temple.

The Oak Creek shooting in 2012 was investigated as a hate crime against the Sikh community, but no motive was released.

In Charleston, South Carolina, Dylann Roof carried out a mass shooting at an African American church on June 17, 2015. The Emanuel African Methodist Episcopal Church was a center of the community and has played a role in the fight for civil rights since the days of slavery. Roof, a white man, attacked the church during a bible study group, killing nine and wounding a tenth parishioner.

Unlike in many mass shootings, Roof was taken into custody by police and was put on trial. Investigators also found that Roof had published what they called a "manifesto," which outlined his racist views and motivations for the attack. He also confessed to investigators that he had committed the shooting and told them he hoped to spark "a race war." Although the attack was investigated as an act of terrorism, Roof was eventually charged with hate crimes and convicted on all counts.

Both of these attacks raised a debate about hate groups and violence motivated by racism or other biases. Roof and Page were connected to or held the same beliefs as white supremacist groups, many of which advocate for violence against people of color or those of non-Christian faiths. Sikhs, many of whom are of Indian descent, wear turbans similar to those worn by some Muslims, which gave rise to concerns that Page was targeting the temple due to Islamophobia, or the fear and hatred of Muslims.

These two shootings, which seem to have had political motivations behind them, were not designated as terrorist attacks. This makes some people question why two such hate crimes do not meet the threshold for terrorist activity. Some critics have suggested that it was due to the misconception that Islamist attacks are the only ones that qualify as terrorism, while those carried out by white Americans are seen as isolated incidents.

Pulse Nightclub and San Bernardino

On June 12, 2016, Omar Mateen carried out a mass shooting at the Pulse nightclub in Orlando, Florida. During the attack he killed forty-nine people—primarily lesbian, gay, bisexual, transgender, and queer (LGBTQ) and Latino victims—and himself while wounding fifty-three others. This wide scope made it the largest mass shooting carried out by a single shooter, the largest domestic terrorist attack to take place since the September 11 attacks on the World Trade Center and the Pentagon, and the deadliest attack against the LGBTQ community in US history.

The Pulse nightclub shooting was the largest recent mass shooting in United States history, as well as the largest violent attack against the LGBTQ community.

Mateen called 911 himself and told the responder that he was loyal to the terrorist organization the Islamic State in Iraq and Syria (ISIS). He also told negotiators that he was carrying out the attack in response to the United States' campaign against ISIS in Iraq and Syria. Although the FBI has found no direct connection between Mateen and ISIS, statements made by the group in the days following the attack expressed their support for Mateen's actions and called him a "soldier of the caliphate."

Another shooting ISIS expressed similar support for was the 2015 San Bernardino shooting during which a married couple, Syed Rizwan Farook and Tashfeen Malik, killed fourteen and injured twenty-two at a local public health facility's holiday party. Although they did not express their support for ISIS prior to the attack, an FBI investigation found that they had done so through private messages to each other. FBI agents also found other online evidence of their support for extremist ideologies. ISIS later expressed their support for the attack on the radio.

Both of these attacks were carried out by American Muslims (Malik was a permanent resident while both Farook and Mateen were American-born citizens) who are believed to have been radicalized over the course of multiple years through the Internet. But none of them are believed to have had direct contact with ISIS, which means that ISIS did not help plan or carry out either of the attacks. The willingness of ISIS to express support or claim credit for such attacks has made it difficult to determine whether these attacks should be considered the work of this terrorist organization or isolated incidents motivated by extremism. These attacks have also raised questions about how best to combat radicalization.

CHAPTER THREE

The Psychology of Mass Shootings

Understanding why someone would carry out a mass shooting is difficult in part because most attackers die before they make their intentions or motives clear. This leaves it to experts, the media, the public, and the government to sort through the evidence left behind and draw conclusions that could help save lives by identifying possible future threats. But doing so is not easy, and it requires an understanding of many underlying issues, such as cultural isolation, the role of mental health, and the process of radicalization. This requires an in-depth look at certain psychological factors that may motivate mass shooters.

Mass Shooters

Although there are differences between all mass shooters, counterterrorism expert and Rutgers professor John Cohen has been researching mass shootings for many years and has identified patterns among those who carry out attacks.

"They seem to be people who come from dysfunctional families, who feel disconnected from the community, who have suffered a series of life failures. They may have some criminal history or some history of mental health issues," Cohen told National Public Radio (NPR) in 2015. "They're looking for something to give their life cause. And unfortunately, what we have seen, in particular, over the past several years, is ... more and more

Researchers have tried to understand what motivates mass shooters, but similarities aren't always easy to find.

people seem to be focusing on conducting mass casualty attacks as that mechanism for bringing purpose to their life."

This sense of disconnect with their community is one of the key commonalities among mass shooters. They are often described as loners who kept to themselves, didn't quite fit in, or otherwise felt isolated. Cohen and other experts have found that this can make someone susceptible to ideologies like those promoted by ISIS or white nationalist groups. These extremist organizations are able to manipulate that sense of isolation and make an individual feel as if they belong to a larger community, and eventually they may be able to motivate that person to carry out an attack. This process is called radicalization.

In some cases, however, radicalization is done without any contact. Self-radicalization can take place when someone has access to propaganda promoting extremism. Omar Mateen and Dylann Roof are both examples of shooters who are believed to have self-radicalized. Mateen pledged his support for ISIS without any known contact with the group, while Roof supported white nationalist groups without having any direct links with those organizations. Self-radicalized individuals pose a unique threat because they are less likely to be noticed by law enforcement officials monitoring things like social media accounts linked to terrorist groups or individuals traveling to countries where groups like ISIS are active. It then becomes difficult to know how to identify and watch individuals at risk of self-radicalization without infringing on personal privacy.

Radicalization is believed to turn to violence when an individual feels they have been wronged. This usually takes a specific incident, but it can be something small. "It could be something in the workplace. It could be some other type of life event which serves as the catalyst for them becoming violent," Cohen told NPR.

This sense of being wronged can be seen in many of the mass shootings discussed in the previous chapter. Dylann Roof specifically targeted a church attended by people of color because he believed they were infringing on the rights of white people. Fort Hood shooter Nidal Hasan carried out his attack after a workplace dispute. Virginia Tech shooter Seung-Hui Cho is believed to have had a romantic interest in one of his first victims, who did not return his feelings. These incidents, though small inconveniences for most, can become the motivator for violence among those who carry out mass shootings.

Mass shooter Dylann Roof targeted an African-American church due to white supremacist beliefs.

Mental Health

Following mass shootings there are often calls for easier access to mental health services. Mass shooters are often assumed to have a mental illness given the level of violence they engage in, although this is not always the case. According to the National Institute of Health (NIH), around 60 percent of those who carried out mass shootings showed some signs of possible mental illness. It is important to point out that showing signs of mental illness is not the same thing as having a diagnosed mental illness, and research has shown that those who are diagnosed are more likely to be victims than perpetrators of violent crime. The same NIH report also notes that "the notion that mental illness causes gun violence stereotypes a vast and diverse population of persons diagnosed with psychiatric conditions and oversimplifies links between violence and mental illness."

Few would argue that better access to mental health services is a bad thing, and in some cases it might help identify issues like paranoia

HOW MASS SHOOTERS GET THEIR WEAPONS

One of the first questions asked after a mass shooting is how the shooter had access to a firearm and whether or not they bought the gun legally. It is widely believed that guns sold illegally account for a significant portion of gun crime, but this idea is hard to verify since few weapons used in violent crime are recovered. But in the case of mass shootings, that proves largely false. Studies have found that around 80 percent of guns used in mass shootings were bought legally. In some cases, including that of the Charleston church shooting, background checks or facts admitted by the shooters themselves should have excluded them from buying a firearm, but sellers did not stop them. In other cases, such as the Sandy Hook shooting, guns were in the home of the shooter but did not belong to them. The person legally approved to own these guns was not the person to use them in the attacks.

or depression that could lead to mass shootings. But too often mental illness becomes the focus of discussions that fail to take into account the larger context for shootings. Because of this, comprehensive solutions are not found. It also puts pressure on mental health providers to identify possible threats and decide who should or should not have guns, which is a demand that unfairly suggests they are responsible for later acts of violence.

According to the NIH, many people use stereotypes of mental illness to diagnose mass shooters after the fact, which leads to increased stigma against those who live with mental health issues. These populations are more likely to be victimized than to carry out violent crime, and understanding that is an important step in protecting them and making sure the rights of such individuals are not infringed upon.

Issues Around Mass Shootings

M ass shootings are complex tragedies that raise many questions. The issues that influence mass shootings and the debate around how to fight them are some of the most important discussions of our time. Although most people agree that gun violence must be dealt with, these issues make it difficult to reach agreement on how to move forward.

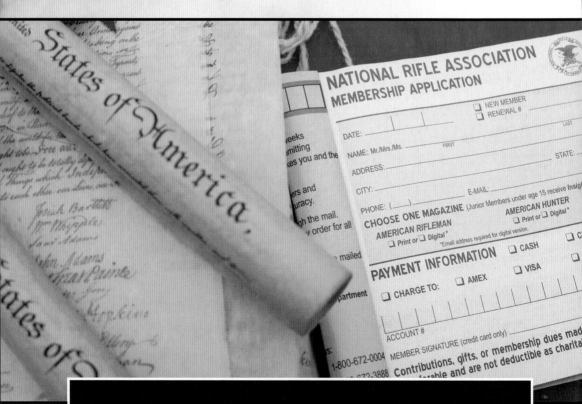

Interpretations of the Second Amendment are varied, which makes it difficult to agree on the Constitution's role in gun control.

The Second Amendment

In the debate surrounding mass shootings and gun violence, the Second Amendment is one of the first thoughts in many people's minds. This is with good reason—the Second Amendment outlines the rights of the people to own "arms," or firearms, and is part of the Bill of Rights. But it is also brief, and there are many different interpretations of the right it provides. As written and ratified in 1791, it reads, "A well regulated militia being necessary to the security of a free State, the right of the people to keep and bear Arms shall not be infringed."

There is much debate about what this means and how it should be applied to legislation. Advocates for gun reform interpret it to mean that while the right to own guns is part of the US Constitution, the Second Amendment does not inhibit the government from providing some limitations on that ownership through background checks and other regulations. Some point to the mention of a "well regulated militia" as suggesting that the Founding Fathers did not intend for all individuals to have unchecked access to firearms, particularly because the militias that existed in the late 1700s eventually became the modern National Guard.

But those who oppose reform believe the Second Amendment should be read literally and that the state should have no or very little interference in gun ownership. Groups such as the NRA believe that gun ownership is one of the first means by which the people combat tyranny and that private ownership of firearms is a way to protect the people from overreaching government ambitions. Although some who advocate for this reading of the Second Amendment do support limited reform, including background checks, many do not support banning specific types of firearms or providing national regulations.

This wide interpretation makes finding solutions to the ongoing debate difficult. The Constitution itself is a source of contention between those who feel the Founding Fathers' words should be read literally and those who feel it should be interpreted in a way that accounts for modern issues and norms. While many countries have adapted or rewritten their constitutions—and the states do so from time to time—the US Constitution has only been updated through amendments since it was written in the late 1700s. Like the rest of the Constitution, the Second Amendment thus becomes part of a larger discussion on the role of our founding documents in the modern age.

Personal Privacy

Another issue surrounding mass shootings and how to respond to them is personal privacy. This applies to proposed reforms and current attempts to mitigate gun violence, such as background checks and a gun-owner database, as well as ways we can prevent mass shootings through monitoring. Groups including the American Civil Liberties Union (ACLU) have expressed concern over proposed options that could quickly infringe on the personal privacy of individuals.

Among the proposed legislative reforms that groups and lawmakers have put forward, the idea of any kind of database has drawn the most concern from advocates for personal freedom and privacy. Gun owner registration laws vary by state, and there is no nationwide system that tracks ownership. The ACLU and others have raised concern that such a database, even if created just to maintain an idea of where the country's roughly 300 million guns are, could be used for programs that infringe on privacy. This is a concern that has become even more pronounced as worries about national surveillance increase.

The terrorist attacks on September 11, 2001 sparked a national debate on how to best monitor potential threats.

In the case of potential terrorist attacks, finding a way to effectively track possible threats while respecting the privacy of individuals has been an ongoing debate since the days following September 11, 2001. Although the Patriot Act of 2001 granted the government powers that enhanced their ability to monitor those inside and outside the United States, there are concerns that such surveillance can be racist, can turn to profiling Muslims, and does not effectively address all potential threats.

The ways in which the government and law enforcement identify potential threats has been called into question as mass shootings continue to occur. But balancing personal privacy and the need to identify threats before they take place is largely seen as incompatible. Few answers have been offered as to how these two important aspects of fighting terrorism can be reconciled.

Radicalization

One of the biggest questions in the fight against international terrorism is how people are radicalized. In the age of the Internet, it is easier than ever

SOCIAL MEDIA AND RADICALIZATION

The Internet has made it easier than ever for people around the world to connect and communicate. But it has also proven a useful recruiting tool for hate groups and terrorist organizations. White nationalists have long used Internet forums to organize and communicate, and more recently ISIS has developed an expansive social media presence that allows them to talk to possible recruits around the world. ISIS uses popular sites such as Facebook and Twitter to contact and influence those who might join their organization. Although their accounts are often deleted, they create new ones just as quickly. It has also proven difficult to stop the spread of their propaganda online. This means that the group is able to use popular platforms to radicalize supporters, and people who find their information online can self-radicalize.

for hateful or violent ideologies to be found by people who feel isolated or disenfranchised, and that connection can lead to attacks. Although mass shootings and other attacks appear to be the problem, they are often a symptom of a much larger problem that is difficult to combat.

Radicalization is the process that takes place when someone becomes extreme in their views, which often advocate for violence. Although the word is often associated with Islamist terrorism, radicalization can also refer to people becoming part of white supremacist groups, ethnic hate groups, or other organizations that are based around political, social, or racial differences. People who are radicalized are often talked about as if they have been brainwashed or have a mental illness, but studies have found that this isn't usually the case. Rather, the process of radicalization is a complex and time-consuming one, and many of those who are radicalized feel they are outsiders or are looking for meaning. Those who seek to radicalize people can manipulate those emotions and make possible recruits feel connected to a larger mission. This can be done online or in person and can take many months—or even years—of sustained and regular contact.

CHAPTER FIVE

How Can We Fight Mass Shootings?

There are many ideas and opinions on how to best combat mass shootings and fight radicalization. Suggestions from experts range from reforming gun legislation to ways individuals can help stop radicalization. While suggestions might differ, it is important to learn what experts think about how mass shootings can be prevented, as well as the links between mass shootings and terrorism.

Mass Shootings Versus Terrorism

As we saw in Chapter Two, not all mass shootings are formally labeled as terrorism. This is for many reasons, including issues raised by putting people on trial for terrorism rather than murder or assault. When is a mass shooting an act of terrorism? The answer is complicated.

By definition, terrorism is an act of violence against civilians to achieve a political goal through fear. In some cases, mass shooters make clear what their goals are, whether it is Dylann Roof starting "a race war" or Syed Rizwan Farook and Tashfeen Malik carrying out retribution on behalf of ISIS. But since some of these shooters are believed to have had no contact with the groups they supported, the actual impact of such groups is limited. Lone attackers and where they fit in the network of terrorist organizations is something we struggle to understand, as shown by our lack of agreement about whether or not they are terrorists.

Partisanship about gun control and mass shootings has made it difficult to reach an agreement on how to stop attacks.

Such labels matter. If we do consider these lone attacks as acts of terrorism, then we are accepting that the ability of groups, such as ISIS or white nationalists, to carry out attacks in the United States is growing. Confronting mass shootings as acts of terrorism would also mean changing law enforcement tactics to be potentially more invasive, as we will discuss in the next chapter. If mass shootings are considered terrorism, it could mean that hundreds of acts of terrorism are carried out each year, a crisis that suggests more connection between attacks than there actually is.

That being said, understanding how people decide to carry out mass shootings does intersect with research into terrorism. Even if we do not consider each mass shooting an act of terrorism, it is a tactic that uses fear to promote a worldview or cause by targeting civilians. Therefore, these two issues run parallel even if they are not the same thing.

Counterterrorism

Counterterrorism policy is complicated and particularly difficult to implement because it has to be forward thinking rather than just responding to current threats. To properly fight terrorism at home or abroad, it is important to understand how people are radicalized and what can be done to make terrorist organizations less powerful. In recent years, experts have also warned that social media can play a role in radicalization around the world as it gives organizations access to possible recruits who they would otherwise never be able to contact.

To fight propaganda from terrorist organizations, experts suggest campaigns that spell out how negative and violent hate groups such as ISIS are, as well as efforts to make sure members of isolated or marginalized populations feel they are part of a larger community. This can

CONCEALED CARRY

Concealed carry is a controversial policy that has been adopted across the country. Although it varies across state lines, it allows people to apply for permits to carry a concealed, or hidden, weapon. In some states it is as simple as filling out the appropriate paperwork, while in other states there must be a demonstrated need to carry the weapon or other requirements that must be met. In late 2016, it was announced that a bill legalizing concealed carry at a national level would be put before Congress in 2017. Supporters intend for the policy to allow more trained and armed individuals in the community to defend themselves and others against shooters or other threats. But critics have expressed concern that concealed carry would put more people in danger if it lacked the proper training and vetting of those trying to intervene in an active shooter situation.

stop people who might otherwise look for connection with such groups while making clear that the ideology of these groups is negative.

In 2016, Karen Greenberg, the director of Fordham University's Center on National Security, also advocated for programs in the community that can engage with people who do not pose an immediate terrorist threat but could do so in the future. "This type of organization would be embedded in civil society and deal with individuals who are on the verge of going down the path that we know can lead to violence," she told the Council on Foreign Relations.

Gun Control

How legislation can be used to stop mass shootings is the subject of heated debate. Some advocates for greater restrictions on gun ownership argue that by reducing potential attackers' access to weapons, we can at least limit their ability to kill others. But those opposed to greater restrictions feel such regulation would infringe on the rights of lawful gun owners to use firearms for recreation and self-defense. Finding a middle ground where both sides are happy has proven difficult.

Some possible solutions proposed by advocates and lawmakers who support what has popularly been called "common sense gun reform" are restrictions on certain ammunition and weapons, such as high-capacity magazines and armor-piercing ammunition, and a longer waiting period before a gun can be purchased. More significant reforms include changing requirements for concealed carry permits to demonstrate need

Although schools in many states are designated as gun-free zones, some lawmakers are unsure that this policy deters shooters.

and requiring firearms to be kept outside of the home or locked away when inside of a home. Background checks for all purchases are more widely agreed upon, but this reform has not yet been adopted.

Meanwhile, those opposed to greater gun restrictions have questioned the effectiveness of gun-safe zones, such as schools, and have advocated for more widespread gun ownership to allow people to defend themselves. They also have suggested that teachers and school officials should be trained to use firearms in an active shooter situation and that individuals should intervene to protect others against potential threats.

There are concerns raised by all these suggestions. Advocates for gun ownership are concerned that greater regulation would make it more difficult for people to defend themselves, while those who support greater reforms are concerned that increasing the number of guns in circulation could lead to more shootings. It is also unclear if individual gun owners are properly trained to respond to an active shooter situation or what impact more firearms could have on the learning environment in schools.

The Media

For decades, people have questioned the role of the media in promoting violence. Although there is no conclusive evidence that media coverage of

PARENTAL
ADVISORY
EXPLICIT CONTENT

The **Parental Advisory**
is a notice to parents
that recordings identified
by this logo may contain strong language
or depictions of violence,
sex or substance abuse.
Parental discretion is advised.

Many are concerned about the impact of violent imagery in popular culture and worry it could motivate shooters.

mass shootings has an impact on future attacks, many are still concerned that the media plays a harmful role by giving mass shooters attention and encouraging a culture of violence that desensitizes people. Some have suggested that the media should not focus so intently on mass shootings or that violence in video games and other entertainment should be restricted.

But these solutions also pose concerns about free speech and the right to information. The media do shape the way we understand mass shootings, and in some cases media outlets report inaccurate information when little is known. This is damaging and makes it difficult for the public to separate fact from fiction when the situation is better understood. But to stop or heavily limit coverage also robs the public of critical information about the frequency of mass shootings, attackers' motives, and how the country responds. Meanwhile, restricting what can be shown on television and in movies raises concerns about where to draw the line and what that kind of censorship could mean for artists in the future.

There are no easy answers in the debate over how to combat mass shootings, but it is clear that progress requires widespread agreement and a comprehensive approach that takes into account access to firearms, the rights of individuals, and what leads individuals to carry out such attacks.

CHAPTER SIX

The Future of Mass Shootings

Terrorism is an ever-changing and evolving threat with terrorist organizations responding quickly to the world around them. Mass shootings are also always evolving as new technology becomes available to the public. As we've seen, finding solutions to end mass

The Brady Campaign to Prevent Gun Violence is one of the nation's largest gun control lobby groups.

shootings might seem far off at this time, and mass shootings are likely to be an issue facing the United States for years to come. But as terrorism evolves, what role will mass shootings play in the strategy used by terrorist organizations?

According to the statistics website FiveThirtyEight, domestic terrorist attacks with guns are a larger threat to security in the United States than foreign terrorism. We've discussed already how difficult it is to determine whether a shooting is or is not a terrorist attack, but research by the Global Terrorism Database found that every terrorist attack on US soil between 2015 and 2016 was carried out with firearms.

POLITICS AND THE FUTURE OF MASS SHOOTINGS

Politics play a large role in the debate about mass shooting and terrorism, and this often makes it difficult for solutions to be reached. Lobbying efforts by groups such as the National Rifle Association and the Brady Campaign to Prevent Gun Violence provide financial incentives for politicians on both sides of the gun control debate, and in turn, politicians have added to an environment in which both sides are cast as enemies. Given the complexity of these issues, it's important

Islamic extremism is one possible ideology that could motivate mass shooters to carry out attacks.

that both sides of the political divide come together to find effective solutions. But politics makes that difficult and has led to the stalemate we've seen in recent years.

As we've seen, there are concerns that groups like ISIS are able to recruit US citizens or inspire attacks carried out in their name. This is a significant threat that is believed to increase as ISIS loses control of its territory in the Middle East. Recent attacks in Europe, which were orchestrated by ISIS supporters, could signal that the group is seeking to motivate attacks on foreign soil rather than luring supporters to fight for them in Syria, Iraq, and other countries. If this is true, then it is possible that ISIS might use mass shootings as a means to harm the United States from afar through radicalizing people online. However, so-called "homegrown," or US-based, terrorism remains an equally grave threat and, as we've seen, is not limited to a particular ideology or religion.

There are still so many questions surrounding mass shootings in the United States. Finding answers will require hard work, compromise, and a comprehensive approach that takes into account the many concerns and issues we've discussed. If this is accomplished, the United States might be able to effectively combat mass shootings—both as acts of terrorism and as lone attacks.

Timeline

1791 The Second Amendment is ratified as part of the Bill of Rights.

1966 The first modern mass shooting is carried out by Charles Whitman at the University of Texas in Austin.

1977 Harlon Carter takes over leadership of the National Rifle Association (NRA), which leads to a policy change that advocates for no compromise on gun reforms.

1993 The Brady Handgun Violence Prevention Act requires background checks on some firearm sales.

1994 The Federal Assault Weapons Ban bars the sale of semiautomatic assault weapons; this expires in 2004 without being renewed.

1997 Congress passes a bill restricting the Centers for Disease Control's ability to research gun violence and mass shootings.

1999 Eric Harris and Dylan Klebold carry out a mass shooting at Columbine High School on April 20.

2005 The Protection of Lawful Commerce in Arms Act bars manufacturers and dealers from being held liable on account of negligence for crimes committed with weapons they sell.

2007 Seung-Hui Cho carries out a mass shooting at Virginia Tech on April 16.

2009 Nidal Hasan carries out a mass shooting at Fort Hood on November 5.

► **2012** Wade Michael Paige carries out a mass shooting at a Sikh temple in Oak Creek, Wisconsin, on August 5; Adam Lanza carries out a mass shooting at Sandy Hook Elementary School in Newtown, Connecticut, on December 14.

► **2013** President Obama signs an executive order with twenty-three gun control measures.

► **2014** Ivan Lopez carries out another mass shooting at Fort Hood on April 2.

► **2014** The Islamic State in Iraq and Syria (ISIS) becomes a prominent terrorist organization in the Middle East and begins recruiting foreign fighters.

► **2015** Dylann Roof carries out a mass shooting at Emanuel African Methodist Episcopal Church on June 17; Syed Rizwan Farook and Tashfeen Malik carry out a shooting in San Bernardino, California, on December 2; the Supreme Court refuses to hear a case on an assault weapons ban.

► **2016** Omar Mateen carries out the largest mass shooting in US history at Pulse nightclub on June 12.

Glossary

background check Using a national or state system to look at criminal records or other sources that could indicate if an individual poses a threat.

Brady Campaign to Prevent Gun Violence An advocacy organization founded in 1974 to promote gun control as a solution to end gun violence.

caliphate A region historically ruled over by an Islamic ruler, called a caliph, now adopted as a term by ISIS for their territories.

domestic terrorism Attacks carried out by US citizens on American soil rather than by foreign nationals.

duels In history, a way to settle arguments by having two people shoot at each other from an agreed-upon distance.

extremism Beliefs that are outside the norm for political or social views, which are often pursued aggressively or violently.

gun violence Any act of violence carried out with a gun.

hate crime A crime targeting a person because of their race, sexuality, gender, or other identifier.

high-capacity magazines A firearm magazine, or ammunition-storing device, that can hold a large amount of ammunition.

ideology Opinions or stances based on political, cultural, or religious beliefs.

imam A Muslim leader who leads prayers.

Islamic State in Iraq and Syria (ISIS) A terrorist organization that grew out of al-Qaeda in Iraq and gained large swaths of territory across Iraq and Syria beginning in 2014.

mass shootings A shooting in which four or more indiscriminately chosen people are killed.

National Rifle Association (NRA) An organization founded in 1871 to advocate for the rights of gun owners.

radical Islam Organizations or groups that use Islamic belief to justify violence.

radicalization The process by which an individual becomes a supporter of extremist political or social views.

social norms Unwritten rules of behavior that a society upholds but can change over time.

stalemate A situation in which neither side can move forward or make progress.

terrorism When a group or individual uses fear to achieve political goals.

vigilante justice When a private individual takes it upon themselves to apply the law.

white nationalist groups Organizations that promote an ideology that calls for separation of races and/or the supremacy of white individuals.

For More Information

The Brady Campaign to Prevent Gun Violence
840 First Street, NE, Suite 400
Washington, DC 20002
(202) 370-8100
Website: http://www.bradycampaign.org
The Brady Campaign is a leading advocate for measures to prevent mass
    shootings and gun violence.

Canadian Coalition for Firearm Rights
PO Box 91572
Mer Bleu PO
Ottawa, ON, Canada K1W0A6
(844) 243-2237
Website: http://www.firearmrights.ca
This organization advocates for the rights of gun owners in Canada.

Canadian Network for Research on Terrorism, Security, and Society
Department of Sociology and Legal Studies
University of Waterloo
PAS Building, Room 2045
200 University Avenue West
Waterloo, ON, Canada N2L3G1
(519) 888-4567
Website: http://www.tsas.ca
Based out of the University of Waterloo in Canada, this research center
    studies terrorism in Canada and around the world.

Center for the Study of Terrorism at the Foreign Policy Research Institute
1528 Walnut Street, Suite 610
Philadelphia, PA 19102
(215) 732-3774
Website: http://www.fpri.org/research/terrorism
The Center for the Study of Terrorism at the Foreign Policy Research
    Institute conducts in-depth research on terrorism and how to
    prevent attacks.

Everytown for Gun Safety
PO Box 4184
New York, NY 10163
Website: http://everytown.org
Everytown for Gun Safety is a nonprofit organization that advocates for
    gun control and against gun violence. The organization works with the
    press and the public, as well as lobbying congress, for common sense
    measures, such as background checks on all firearms purchases.

The John Hopkins Center for Gun Policy and Research
615 N. Wolfe Street
Baltimore, MD 21205
Website: http://www.jhsph.edu/research/centers-and-institutes
    /johns-hopkins-center-for-gun-policy-and-research
Based at John Hopkins University, the John Hopkins Center for
    Gun Policy and Research is dedicated to reducing gun-related
    injuries and deaths through implementing policy based on research
    and public health principles.

The National Rifle Association (NRA)
11250 Waples Mill Road
Fairfax, VA 22030
(800) 672-3888
Website: http://www.nra.org
The NRA is a leading advocate for the rights of gun owners. It is the oldest
    continously operating civil rights organization in the United States and
    is one of the most influential lobbying groups in the country.

Websites

Because of the changing nature of Internet links, Rosen Publishing has
developed an online list of websites related to the subject of this book. This
site is updated regularly. Please use this link to access the list:

http://www.rosenlinks.com/TER21/massshoot

For Further Reading

Cefrey, Holly. *Gun Violence: Violence and Society* (Violence and Society). New York, NY: Rosen Publishing, 2009.

Gabor, Thomas. *Confronting Gun Violence in America*. New York, NY: Palgrave Macmillan, 2016.

Giffords, Gabrielle and Mark Kelly. *Enough: Our Fight to Keep America Safe from Gun Violence.* New York, NY: Scribner, 2014.

Hasday, Judy L. *Forty-Nine Minutes of Madness: The Columbine High School Shooting* (Disasters—People in Peril). New York, NY: Enslow Publishing, 2012.

Klarevas, Louis. *Rampage Nation: Securing America from Mass Shootings.* Amherst, NY: Prometheus Books, 2016.

Mooney, Carla. *Domestic Terrorism* (Hot Topics). Farmington Hills, MI: Lucent Books, 2014.

Nakaya, Andrea C. *Thinking Critically: Mass Shootings* (Thinking Critically). San Diego, CA: ReferencePoint Press, 2015.

Schmermund, Elizabeth. *Domestic Terrorism* (At Issue). New York, NY: Greenhaven Publishing, 2017.

Streissguth, Tom. *District of Columbia v. Heller: The Right to Bear Arms Case* (Landmark Supreme Court Cases). New York, NY: Enslow Publishing, 2011.

Torres, John Albert. *The People Behind School Shootings and Public Massacres* (Psychology of Mass Murderers). New York, NY: Enslow Publishing, 2016.

Wolny, Philip. *Gun Rights: Interpreting the Constitution* (Understanding the United States Constitution). New York, NY: Rosen Publishing, 2015.

Woolf, Alex. *Terrorism* (Global Issues). New York, NY: Rosen Publishing, 2011.

Bibliography

Berkowitz, Bonnie et al. "The Math of Mass Shootings." *The Washington Post*, July 27, 2016. https://www.washingtonpost.com/graphics/national/mass-shootings-in-america.

Bialek, Carl. "Terrorists Are Turning to Guns More Often in U.S. Attacks." *FiveThirtyEight*, June 12, 2016. http://fivethirtyeight.com/features/terrorists-are-turning-to-guns-more-often-in-u-s-attacks.

Bjelopera, Jerome P. "American Jihadist Terrorism: Combating a Complex Threat." *Congressional Research Service*, January 23, 2013. https://fas.org/sgp/crs/terror/R41416.pdf.

Bjelopera, Jerome P. "Domestic Terrorism Appears to Be Reemerging as a Priority at the Department of Justice." *Congressional Research Service*, August 15, 2014. https://fas.org/sgp/crs/terror/IN10137.pdf.

Bjelopera, Jerome P. "Sifting Domestic Terrorism from Hate Crime and Homegrown Violent Extremism." *Congressional Research Service*, June 13, 2016. https://fas.org/sgp/crs/terror/IN10299.pdf.

Bump, Philip. "Radical Islam Accounts for Few Recent Mass Shootings But Also Some of the Deadliest." *The Washington Post*, June 12, 2016. https://www.washingtonpost.com/news/the-fix/wp/2016/06/12/islamic-terrorism-accounts-for-few-recent-mass-shootings-but-also-some-of-the-deadliest/?utm_term=.e8e5421dd090.

Hyman, Ira. "The Orlando Mass Shootings: Terrorist Attack or Hate Crime?" *Psychology Today*, June 20, 2016. https://www.psychologytoday.com/blog/mental-mishaps/201606/the-orlando-mass-shooting-terrorist-attack-or-hate-crime.

Krouse, William J. and Daniel J. Richardson. "Mass Murder with Firearms: Incidents and Victims, 1999-2013." *Congressional Research Service*,

July 30, 2015. https://fas.org/sgp/crs/misc/R44126.pdf.

Lavergne, Gary M. A *Sniper in the Tower: The Charles Whitman Murders*. Denton, TX: University of North Texas Press, 1997.

Macleish, Kenneth T. and Jonathan M. Metzi. "Mental Illness, Mass Shootings, and the Politics of American Firearms." *American Journal of Public Health*, February 2015. https://www.ncbi.nlm.nih.gov/pmc /articles/PMC4318286.

Marche, Stephen. "Why We Shouldn't Call Recent Mass Shootings Terrorism." *Esquire*, July 30, 2015. http://www.esquire.com /news-politics/a36768/terrorism-shootings.

Masters, Jonathan. "Foiling the Next U.S. Mass Shooting." *Council on Foreign Relations*, June 13, 2016. http://www.cfr.org/counterterrorism /foiling-next-us-mass-shooting/p37950.

Oldham, Abbey. "2015: The year of mass shootings." *PBS Newshour*, January 1, 2016. http://www.pbs.org/newshour /rundown/2015-the-year-of-mass-shootings.

"The Psychology of Radicalization: How Terrorist Groups Attract Young Followers." *NPR*, December 15, 2015. http://www.npr .org/2015/12/15/459697926/the-psychology-of-radicalization -how-terrorist-groups-attract-young-followers.

Ruane, Kathleen Ann. "The Advocacy of Terrorism on the Internet: Freedom of Speech Issues and the Material Support Statutes." *Congressional Research Service*, September 8, 2016. https://fas.org/sgp/crs /terror/R44626.pdf.

"A Study of Active Shooter Incidents in the United States Between 2000 and 2013." *FBI*, January 10, 2013. https://www.fbi.gov/file/active -shooter-study-2000-2013-1.pdf.

Index

About the Author

Bridey Heing is a writer and book critic based in Washington, DC. She holds degrees in political science and international affairs from DePaul University and Washington University in Saint Louis. Her areas of focus are comparative politics and Iranian politics. Her masters' thesis explores the evolution of populist politics and democracy in Iran since 1900. She has written about Iranian affairs, women's rights, and art and politics for publications such as *The Economist*, *Hyperallergic*, and *The Establishment*. She also writes about literature and film. She enjoys traveling, reading, and exploring Washington, DC's, many museums.

Photo Credits

Cover © iStockphoto.com/Marccophoto; back cover and interior pages background aleksandr hunta/Shutterstock.com (smoke), Alex Gontar/Shutterstock.com (grunge);p. 5 Mark Makela/Corbis News/Getty Images; p. 7 vchal/Shutterstock.com; p. 10 Shel Hershorn/The LIFE Images Collection/Getty Images; p. 12 Mark Peterson/Corbis Historical/Getty Images; p. 13 Logan Cyrus/AFP/Getty Images; p. 15 Allan Tannenbaum/The LIFE Images Collection/Getty Images; p. 19 Paul J. Richards/AFP/Getty Images; p. 22 Scott Olson/Getty Images; p. 24 John Panella/Shutterstock.com; p. 27 Maksym Dykha/Shutterstock.com; p. 29 Grace Beahm-Pool/Getty Images; p. 32 David Ryder/Getty Images; p. 35 Universal History Archive/Universal Images Group/Getty Images; p. 39 Tom Williams/CQ Roll Call/Getty Images; pp. 42–43 Visions of America/Universal Images Group/Getty Images; pp. 44–45 Shawn Thew/Getty Images; p. 47 T. J. Kirkpatrick/Getty Images; p. 49 Saul Loeb/AFP/Getty Images.

Designer: Nicole Russo-Duca; Editor and Photo Researcher: Elizabeth Schmermund.